I0152343

COLD FIRE

Donna Allard

Cold Fire

Author: Donna Allard (1956 -)
Editor: Ronda Wicks (1965 -)

Cover title 'Cold Fire" and photograph by Jinn Bug,
used with permission.

All rights reserved. No part of this book may be reproduced or
transmitted in any form or by any means without written
permission from the author or photographer.

First Edition.

Copyright © 2019 Donna Allard
ISBN 978-1-9990964-4-1

Library and Archives Canada ID: LD-2019-11349-1

Published by SkyWing Press, Clinton, ON, Canada

Index

understanding your winter

know when dreams
are over
know which to choose
and which choose you.
know you're history
as you float in its dreams,
perceive its form, and
understand its winter.
know the echoed
ancestral choir,
awaken to it
and rest your pen
on the eternal flame.

red leaf
dedicated to Jinn

you are not
forgotten

you are cherished
like a leaf
within the pages

of my heart

women can die gently

dedicated to my late sister Victorine

she escapes
>the moon's sudden monthly death
>
>the sun's fiery obsession

she escapes
>the poets' passionate indigo blots
>
>the terror of reality
>
>the intimacy of history

she escapes
>the hand of perception
>
>the twisted umbilical cord of rebirth

she escapes
>necessity and dies gently
>
>*into thought*

when I die

when I die
cast my face,
purse my lips
in a forever kiss

take the cast and mount it
on the mantel,
fire a candle, watch
my shadow
dance

when you miss me most
lay lavender on the mantel,
fire a candle,
dance until dawn, try
to forgive me

when I die
cast my hand,
let it cradle spring
dandelions
on the mantel,

in its season
a winter cranberry branch,
in summer, beach pebbles,

and in fall, a maple leaf.

forgive me.

when you die request
my mask be
next to yours,
our hands clasped.

take me with you

untwisting

inspired by the work of Igjaffe

untwisting
from
earth

my
third
eye

watching

fire
fire
fire

breathing

pieces
pieces
pieces

kaleidoscope

of
time
of

spaces

of
third
die
mensions

untidaled

find your compass
set sail
cross tidal lines

the garden

we were to meet,
remember?
by the lion waterfall
    3 pm Sunday

you say I never showed,
said the flowers were brilliant
and the lush moss path
    tickled your toes

you left at dusk
when the flower petals closed,
and the lions head trickled
    one last sweet drop

you never asked if I went
I arrived at 2:30
as the high sun lit
    the arched doorway

in a magical moment
I was transformed,
leaping leaf to leaf
    drinking nectar

vanishing into leafy mists

I saw your toes curled over moss,
danced around your shoulders
    you smiled, you waved

I landed gently
on closed petals,
watched the tear being shed
    the moment gone.

the essential other

there are many sweet flowers
and many stones in this garden;
the taller stones named by its dead

a crown of thorns lay hidden
beneath freshly fallen fruit
during autumn's wind

the desire for grace is long gone,
the last rose of the season
shatters under a warm touch

Prophets' words are captive
slaves to otherworldly gods

on a still winter's night
the whisperings of imagination
succumb to frost

the Annecy stone

every now and then
I sit nearby with umbrella in hand
    a notebook
    a Kleenex
    toffee candy

every now and then
loosened by weathered seasons
    a pebble
    a stone
    a leaf

this pen runs blue
like the waters near
    a footbridge
    a shoreline
    a pond

then I remember
    strolling waterways
    aromatic cafes
    welcoming song

then I remember
    the patron's choir
    open hearts

flying like balloons

now I feel
   tears release
   the tides receding
   and an understood quiver

the weathered season
   of my life

sunflower

in memory of environmental activist Gaston Richard

from milky-ways to sea-glass days
your kindness never wavered
summery days and fireside blazes
your love, it never wavered
firefly nights captured in thought
glitter in a time capsule
the earth is flowering
under your fingertips
spiraling hummingbirds
sail forward on your last breath
you stand in the spirit world now
a sunflower towering over
a field of tall grass
waving goodbye
and for now my friend
"goodbye"

sundial

today is a day for a path less travelled,
as Dryas seed-heads
and dragonflies welcome the dawn

just past the pines
is a weathered farm
and generations of toil

I can tell by the sequence
of room additions over time,

the old rose bush's wreath
- no entry -
the chimney is solid like a sundial

I clear the front porch bench
to rest a while, to my left

overgrown apple trees
to my right a path
leads to the creek

a lonely seagull calls
and I must follow, where
old timber lets me cross
the cold teal waters

a blue heron cautiously lands
along a short grass path
combed by moose or deer

the sun is full now,
the Jack pine shade fading

I find a branch for a walking stick
& we venture together

it must be near lunchtime
all of nature setting the table

even ants carrying food to their dens,
woodpeckers chiseling trees
for hidden delicacies
all is right with the world

the Jack pine sundial says
NOON

strolling the blues

standing whitewashed, hidden
behind flowering trees or
floating like a lovers row boat
blues upon blues,
dining nearby
you are savoring local fruits
and *vino molto gustoso*
sitting across: I am
deep in thought
like an ice cube
half-dissolved in whisky
the still high sun
cracking ice

shoot the pen not the poet

I am emotional and superficial and, so what? You can
only go through life by yourself - only you can find
your own way. So what! Yes, I've made a ton of
mistakes and failed at a lot of things, so what?

What do you know about Afghanistan? Kenya? Global
warming? Nothing - only what you've read or been told.
My education might be a sham but I see yours hasn't
been much benefit either.

Egos may be rising now but have you ever fished or
hunted? built a house or solved an economic problem?
You vote for people you would never desire to have as
a close friend. You act out roles trying to fit 'in' only to
realize the suit doesn't fit, and never will. You remit
taxes although you're excluded from government
decisions, why?

You've all become keyboard activists with your virtual
feet firmly planted. You are medical experiments.
Can't handle life? Take a pill will ya?
and be forever lost or worse,
a statistic of unused potential.

Yes I can be rude, a tad arrogant but I can also crack a

good joke. Like you I try to keep in good health and walk enough to see the world in pain.

One night I went to the liquor store only to find frustrated white-skinned people, I drove away half-frightened by what I saw: disconcerted over the deep despair being ritualistically carried like a torch and I, not wanting to be burned, *was*. I drowned that night in a glass of wine.

This is who I am: a poet when I write but an uncivil servant when I don't. This ink is my bloodline. I have no other children, just this, so these pages are the truth as I know it to be. The truth often lies.

I am only a poet when I write. I might give service to a civil word but not now, not here where I tell everyone to GO TO HELL!

Ahhh, it is morning and the dream has only begun.

sacred pond

having walked these mist-ridden shores
a thousand times, watched its tides
under many moon's glow, travelled
its oceans on sails of thought,
i've finally come to recognize
that you are not here. i have missed
our tranquil star gazing, our sea shell
castle constructions, beachcombing
for lost treasures, and sunday ice cream

now I stare into this sacred pond
with eyes emptied of both sun & moon.
even the stars fall into the unknown,
unlike before, when you were here
and we stuck out our tongues
and they landed on them like dew.
we drank their essence and
the universe unfolded before us.

I will wade into our favourite harbour
so it can drink me in, cover me up
with seaweed & kelp, and rinse away
my pain; praying it becomes warm
when you extend the arms I long for
and welcome me home.

remnants of stones

remnants of stones
uncovered by a harsh plunder
of my walking stick as

indian summer rays point
my direction through golden
brush & blood red leaves

i crouch & fingertip clear
a mossy stone where once
a date and name were etched

and then concealed
someone went to great lengths
for anonymity

a rustle of leaves
and goosebumps

i start to run
as an owl sweeps overhead
its silence is deafening

understanding i'm not the prey
my heart breaks against stone

northward

i stand northward
as a treeline shadow
over a graveyard resting
beneath an autumn quilt

i stand eastward
with rembrandt memories
where you last rested
in my arms

i gather leaves
we once said we would pick
to complete the album
of your life

in defense of heron

i just noticed, window high,
the silhouette of a great blue heron
near a small lagoon that is now the
dusty desolation of a white moon

the eagles and hawks are back
so soon the heron will be too--
shunned by the lagoon,
denied in its absence, and
will watch the dark forest defoliate
right before its eyes

seeking refuge from the wind,
it will shatter the mirror underfoot,
the shards will gut rotting fish below
while the great red reflection
bleeds through, undeniable
against the pure snow banking

ghost
inspired by a photo by Andreas Gripp

i see the ghost
in the far wall mirror
adjacent to the bathroom

it is holding a camera
click click focus focus
thought flash

i see you standing there
your kind eyes oblivious to
this memory's lingering
corpse.

remembering yesterday

dedicated to poet Joe Blades

remembering yesterday
leafing through your life
big ring hard cover binder
wordplay 2013 shetland islands

tickets, posters, sticky notes,
scribbling, calendar, photos of locals,
beer labels, historical ruins,
shepherd and his sheep

you manage to guard your grounds,
those familiar maples, as you travel from
valley to hilltop, breathing in & out the
yesterdays & 'morrows

every other page stores a maple leaf,
hues of autumn, a seasoned gift in case
of a chance meeting with someone
who travelled before you--
a promised reminder of home

the wait

the walls of stone
that surround this heart
are plumes of cracked ivory,
chipped sea-greens, broken blues,
brushed with turquoise and tears.
i too, am painted
with painfully stroked feathers
and torn claws.
all my doors are visible
under moonlight, invisible
under glares of unwelcomed eyes.
the pebble path, worn down
by my nails tearing away
the unwanted obstacles underfoot
keeps warm through every
returning sunrise.
i wait there, on that path,
until you call my name
and all i can do is run,
trying to catch the wind.

rains

lightened horizon
takes my breath away,
slow rumble of thunder
beneath my feet, the silence
it procures

a flag, a full mast with such a
commanding presence
cats run for cover
under the rose bush
it is near,

menacing howls
like wolves in heat
garden of flowers
waiting like somebody's bride

i'm a witness under oath
i claim the 5th
and run with the wild horses
of my past, my ancestral angels

the raindrops pound
like lead balloons

i cling to the gazebo shelter

you loved the sex

you loved the sex
flirting with every virgin,
spectacles lowered like a ph.d's,
with raised brow your words take flight,
reminiscent of a bee questing for nectar

you loved the sex
the journey no doubt a pleasure
and your sultry call was
clearly pinnacle

you loved the sex
your mistress' arms comforted you
like a gown of autumn leaves
a dance into infinity

you loved the sex
while driving that red clay road
where you forfeited life's music
for the crashing of glass
against hard-cocked rock...

one shouldn't flirt with death

moon (haiku)

through wood forest
on frosty wind--
chimes

breath (haiku)

rag weed--
sweet poison
on the war path

a winter's green (haiku)

tucked between fresh snows
a four leaf clover--
wishes come true

love bird

dedicated to my friend Nancy Kelly

with my first small regular coffee
we gathered at the round table at tim horton's
english, french and chiac alphabet soup
being served - you must be alert
or get lost in translation

a seven year old joins us -
his small wings spread for landing, and
the awaiting grandmama, open-winged
& firm in eye contact, smiles,
as his gentle little voice says
  "my love bird"

* *I was very touched by his gesture towards his grandmama,*
   "love bird", so young so loving... I damn near cried...

* *Chiac is a variety of Acadian French heavily mixed and structured with English. The word itself is generally considered a derivation of the name "Shediac", a town in the area. Chiac has been embraced in recent years by some Acadian groups as a living and evolving language, and part of their collective culture.*

no tears

as i scroll my facebook wall
a photo blurb stands out:

"16 year old shot 11 times in Brooklyn NY"

the following photo was a paramilitary
or state police siege
that lasted all weekend,
it is now tuesday
and I only found out today;
they say news travels fast?

it will be a year in june
since i cancelled cable tv;
should i cancel the internet too?

i see your children
and in them i see
all the ones i never had

i pray for those who loved that boy
i pray for those who live in fear, and
i pray for sunnier days--
     ones that shed no tears

creamsicle

the sunset was delicious
like a creamsicle
then it went bright white
and lit all shadows

east easy

sun streams between saluting pines
as salmon dance a mosquito jig
we care for each other unthreatened
by our roles in life, and
this love is liberating
this love is comforting--
dependence is unthinkable

along these shore's piled-stone
snowmen guard unfinished songs
everything is communicating
everything is silent too
abundance is accepted
war and peace don't exist
the concept never considered

east easy democracy must escape
cultivated culture

black robes of night cover all living souls
what happens here will happen
everywhere
this is the future

"friends, there are very few of us left"

king & i

i follow the king fisher river up stream,
the banks populated by large, old boat graves

i don rubber boots and a lumber shirt
my father used to wear, if I didn't
the mosquitoes and black flies
would eat me alive.

i take a bag for collecting beach treasures
and matches to start a campfire
-- the august stars are full of mischief tonight

if i follow the northbound tall-grass dunes
to where still waters lie, silent in my approach
and camera ready, the cemetery will unfold
its mind lamp impressions of al purdy

this curious journey of red-leafed days
and tarred sky "take me spent"

i sometimes mourn this open heart country
of sunflower, daisy, wheat, and barley
its tidal dune maps and star crowned universes
where fossil remains are zodiacal tributes

'though my mind lamp is dim, my heart is open,
neither death nor life nor anything between
can squelch such light, not even drunken stupor,
oh yes I have tried that too

i'm like that grain of sand lifted in winds
and whisked away on a flying carpet
        of dreams

rails & wind

"all aboard!" said the conductor
as the rails screamed like swords in battle

we decided to visit my relatives in montreal
and left moncton at 5pm
i was eight and sat by the window
in the train's berth watching
the late night rays cut the darkness
like search lights on the hunt
leaving me feeling detached;
a lonely leaf in the arctic wind.

i never viewed the world the same
afterwards, not even today
as i watch the most recent storm clouds
surround, conquer and disperse...

these steel cold rails are unmovable.

faith

many times
the foundation
beneath my feet
was destroyed

all that was left
was standing on faith
and the firefly
that greeted me

summer the memories

even though my fortress of
inky words ensure some things
i will never forget

i will light a match and burn
all such leaves that gather
under the summer's hot sun

i shall summer these memories
so every heartbeat rumbles
all pools of healing waters,
wear winter's white linens with
diamonds & frosted breath wreaths
as a sign of rebirth

i will address all seasons in turn
and summer the memories

i

i move forward
like the ocean
one day at a time
i erode the land

strong and relentless
like the biting gale
i travel unnoticed
and melt icecaps, glaciers

tomorrow you will find me
as a drop of acid rain
destroying fields
and streams

and at night
for better or for worse
until death do us part

i will be the air you breathe

the weep of sunflowers

sunflower petals & seed fly north
as southward winds sweep fields
like an old farmer's boom

under wild rose bushes
dry, bloodless leaves thorn-crowned
lie on nature's altar

soon full moon snowfalls will arrive
silent on the shores, and stay
'til the daffodils rise again in spring

in this, the yellow death
beholds a new beauty, and
the want of forever

the seasons

as we age the paths
to follow dwindle,
fewer hands are left
to hold us as we pass
the stage of ripened fruit,
our old tree monuments
are etched with names
now stranded, braided
from seasons that came
some decades before

as we age there seems
less need to question
our rare excursions
over warfaring roots--
those memories that trip
less familiar pilgrims
on 'the seasons'
unwelcome mat

mud bay

starlings mistaken for bats
swarm, circle, settle
on mud bay

sea spent

wrapped
in bearded grass
rolling in seaweed

driftwood

we point
we stare
we sigh

spring stars
dance and fall
to winter's night

seagull echoes

Sweet Reflections

Eve Adam snake apple
paradise soap-opera humanity

If the snake convinced Eve the apple was sweet and
hidden truths lied in its seed could not the snake fool
us too with such delicious temptations?
What if the apple was sweet?
What if it carried no bad seed?

What if we all bit the half truth, the 1/2 truth
remaining today, right now, at this coffee shop:
you-Adam me-Eve you a J-W, a Mormon, a Catholic
and me, a New Age junky?

Aren't we all in paradise now? wearing fake religions
and selling political beliefs inside the abstract illusion?
Our lies are smeared across our sleeves and we wipe
the truth from our lips as if wrung from that juicy f*ing
apple so, if the snake lied, we must be its followers, or
why cloak ourselves in this garment?

I can't say if you taste sour in my mouth or sweet,
only that the snake in my eyes is a little green worm,
easily squished between forefinger and thumb
and that the truth stares back from the mirror of your
reflections too. I know because I've seen it there.

the blue underwood

letter from cousin Yseult Fld

the blue underwood typewriter
sits encased in dust
holding an aged blank page
i press the letter "v"

this evening I found out
my sister may be dead
the news punctuated by a full moon
came in a handwritten letter
from florida

a distant cousin's moulin-rouge-dream
written and sent without a thought

i'm not sure why she included it
when the rest of the letter
was pure delight and charm

now the 'morrow is loaded
with thunder-tear storms
cleansing known and unknowns

my sister's name is "victorine"
i press the letter "v".

the eagle

the eagle has landed
all snakes, rats & night flying
creatures left in a hurry
twas the night of the hunters' moon
and all was still, not even a blast
from a cell phone or laptop,
and nothing was stirring
not even a timmie's coffee,
the dance went on 'til midnight
stars fell into everyone's hands
wise men shed their religion for faith
it was magical and all was right
the manger lit by moonlight
a sign from the heavens
that the eagle had landed

the support of your whisper

dedicated to the Aboriginal voices in Kent County NB,
Canada October 18, 2013

the support of your whisper
crossing the valleys of life
bridges our hands in an
invisible bond, strengthening
wavering loves and hope

a whisper, tickling senses,
breaking down the rickety fencing
that keeps everything apart,
that raised eyebrow,
that slight movement of tongue
and lips waiting for more tender breath,
a whisper's constant reminder
of love sought in autumn,
winter, spring & summer

I behold the constant depth
of heart and soul pounding,
a well-weathered drum

and the beauty of such a beat

walk

it looked a long way away
taking one step seemed forever
soon steps became heartbeats

each fauna a language,
each stone pondered on,
each shaking leaf
an opportunity for trust

it's okay to be vulnerable
to feel vulnerable
nature will comfort you
and soon you will realize

you were never alone.

wolf

today it is official we will be fracked in Kent County NB

i am an optimist
so I'm ok
but for the others
my soul cries out
louder than
the wolf or loon
we must let a love-light
be brighter than
the fracking flame
that will never go out
of the eyes of those
who stood in silence
trying to forgive
their own government
for decisions being made
without the consent
of its citizens

uncharted

i awoke finding a map
written in lipstick
on the kitchen table:

"let's meet under the streetlight
after dusk"

the radio was playing:
'some enchanted evening'

i found my way to the golden sands,
stood beneath the light
and its blood orange glow,
my mind sailing...

i wrote on the map's underside
"some uncharted evening"
and tucked it into a cracked wall

it bled as i set sail

the leaving

i entered the only open door
the street shadow couldn't
hide from the pearly light
of nearby windows. at first
glance I saw the antique cross
strung by silver around your neck
and how the time passed slowly
as your clocktower pupils,
your eyes, read 6:30 p.m.
you rushed to catch a train,
left channel lingering and
that pale light casting itself
on the thrown cross

you arrived from montreal
with a ruby rose--
it blossomed for 11 days
or was it just stagnant,
refusing to weep? I threw it out
an hour after you drove away

there are no petals shed
in this house

the owl

the owl perched
high in spruce
reflects upon
still waters
a wandering dragonfly
between tall weeds
a fish blasts
in full sail
outward into
the known
the owl leeps wildly

all this I see
while staring
into your eyes

Chilean Dreams

I am searching for simplicity and a way of life and have
yet to go out west or west of there I've been south but
not way south to Chile. Some day I will walk every
village and city street in Chile, part raindrops and tears,
decipher their origins during a search for their fallen
poets' dreams.

I will search for deep lost interwoven threads
embedded in language, knit them into a cozy throw to
keep my body warm on cold nights. I will follow the
indigo shadows that cast everyone everywhere even
on moonless nights and find myself among them--
ahhh to dream...

The devolution of humanity has begun. This devolution
is the final frontier and its artifacts are hidden. The
whispering-grapevine-winds tell of a spiritual
awakening, the healing necessary to foster humanity.

I cannot speak the Chilean language and, when
watching TV, I read the prosaic English captions
offered on the bottom of the screen they are well-
meaning translations but the poetry, the heart of
community has no X & Y gene - no translation is
needed when eyes meet, even on television.

A new kind of poetry is flaming the Chilean butternut red horizons - a poetry of exile, a rhythmical accent carved on the fruits of labor, and on devastated walled streets of every village and town... buttoned-lipped hands and a tied-rope bordered exile, bloodshot from the Awakening on this Millennium morning to find the last journey's red wine-tinged cigarette butts laying atop each other in the ashtray after sex.

It's a wonderment, this fresh fruit season, ahhh, one day I drink sweet wine lead by dead poets' whispered ramblings but then I must either travel their passages or linger too long while the wild dogs run.

Wild Dogs On The Run

It's mid-winter now and I am older, living at the
cottage year round; a rebel without a cause chopping
softwood and drinking a beer. My mother died last
summer and I decided to take this time to reevaluate
my life.

A sundog is forming so I put hardwood on the
cutting block. My birthday is nearing, and how will I
celebrate it without mom, get drunk? have friends over
to shoot the shit? Nah, Dad will come to the rescue -
he'll bring filet minion fit for a queen to cook on the
wood stove and celebrate life with sparkling wine.

I need a break from the axe and walk down the beach.
The sundog watches my every move. I glance to the
right and then run with horror, up the steps to the
cottage, fumbling from fear and, with mighty strength
I slam the door shut. The wild dogs are on the run!
Their mouths foaming, their stampede echoing, as
trembling, I wait.

Will they crash through my glass window? They sense
the urgency of the sundog too, and leave as quickly as
they arrived...

strange creatures in a foreign land.

war dance

september strolls
through centennial park
along a muddy path
where I witness the battle zone:
each tree a brilliant flag of colors
each tree a country of its own
its leaves falling one by one
into foreign territory
once waving from lofty boughs
they blend into landscape,
wilting, becoming fossils

reaching into a lottery of leaves,
I pick a winner, and
cut into its surface with the word
        "war"
the ruddy sap on red barely legible
bleeding leafy-veins that make me think
of you, and my parents too

there's a brisk feel to the air today--
the leaves are flitting, dancing about,
soon snowflakes will blanket them
then summer will bring blossoms
and bird song. once again I will
travel to my hometown cemetery

to view the granite thumb marks
that identify you among the dead.
funny how we quarter the years
25 - 50 - 75 - 100 and how
we quarter the seasons too,

how i always dread leaving you
alone in death, but sometimes
i feel nothing and then i dance
like a leaf, i dance-dance-dance.

fire within

some people
are emotional pyromaniacs
    they use negative triggers
    to spark a flame
        that will burn silently
                until it reaches

you!

www.ingramcontent.com/pod-product-compliance
Lightning Source LLC
LaVergne TN
LVHW091210080426
835509LV00006B/917